*Little People,* **BIG DREAMS**®
# COCO CHANEL

# Little People, BIG DREAMS®
# COCO CHANEL

Written by
Maria Isabel Sánchez Vegara

Illustrated by
Ana Albero

Translated by Emma Martinez

**Frances Lincoln**
Children's Books

This is the story of a French girl called Gabrielle. When she was little, Gabrielle lived in an orphanage.

The nuns thought Gabrielle was very strange. She was different and they didn't like it.

Gabrielle *was* different. While the other girls played, she liked to sew with a needle and thread.

When Coco finally went to bed, she dreamt in shapes and patterns. She wanted to make so many things!

One day, Coco made a hat for her friend.
Simple and elegant, it was different to the usual style.

Coco made more and more hats, until she had enough to open a hat shop. Her modern designs surprised the *mademoiselles* in Paris.

One evening at a party, Coco saw that the other ladies weren't dancing. Their corsets were too tight and they could hardly breathe!

So Coco created a brand new style, simple and straight. Her dresses and skirts would be comfortable to wear.

At her first fashion show, some people sneered.
Coco's clothes were too strange and different for them.

But as time went on, Coco showed them that to be stylish you don't need to wear corsets or sparkly sequins. . . .

. . . and being different might make other people think differently, too. That's why everyone now remembers the young Gabrielle as the great designer, Coco Chanel.

# COCO CHANEL

(Born 1883 • Died 1971)

1932

1936

Coco Chanel was one of the most famous fashion designers that ever lived. She was born as Gabrielle Chanel in a charity hospital and grew up in a rundown house in a French town. Following the death of her mother, when Gabrielle was 11 years old she was sent to a strict convent school, where she learnt to sew. After school, she became a seamstress, sewing for a tailor during the day, while in the evenings she sang on stage. It was at this time that she earned the nickname "Coco" from the soldiers in the audience.

1937

1962

In 1908 she became a hat-maker and soon afterward opened her first shop in Paris. Soon she had more shops and started to sell clothes as well as hats. Her simple, elegant designs —which were straighter and shorter than normal, and freed women from corsets—took the world by storm. In 1918 Chanel opened a couture house in 31 Rue Cambon and three years later she unveiled her first perfume, Chanel No 5. She became a worldwide fashion icon and her comfortable, easy-to-wear styles changed women's clothes forever.

Want to find out more about **Coco Chanel**?
Have a read of these great books:

*Different Like Coco* by Elizabeth Matthews
*Coco Chanel: Famous Fashion Designers* by Dennis Abrams
*Chanel Fashion Review: Paper Dolls* by Tom Tierney
If you're in New York, you could even visit the Metropolitan Museum of Art,
where you can see some of Coco's famous outfits!
www.metmuseum.org

Brimming with creative inspiration, how-to projects, and useful information to enrich your everyday life, Quarto Knows is a favourite destination for those pursuing their interests and passions. Visit our site and dig deeper with our books into your area of interest: Quarto Creates, Quarto Cooks, Quarto Homes, Quarto Lives, Quarto Drives, Quarto Explores, Quarto Gifts, or Quarto Kids.

Text copyright © 2014 Maria Isabel Sanchez Vegara. Illustrations copyright © 2014 Ana Albero.
Original concept of the series by Maria Isabel Sánchez Vegara, published by Alba Editorial, s.l.u
Produced under trademark licence from Alba Editorial s.l.u and Beautifool Couple S.L.

First published in Spain in 2014 under the title *Pequeña & Grande Coco Chanel*
by Alba Editorial, s.l.u.
Baixada de Sant Miquel, 1, 08002 Barcelona www.albaeditorial.es

First published in the USA in 2016 by Frances Lincoln Children's Books,
an imprint of The Quarto Group,
100 Cummings Center, Suite 265D, Beverly, MA 01915, USA.
T +1 978-282-9590 F +1 078-283-2742 www.QuartoKnows.com

All rights reserved

No part of this publication may be reproduced, stored in a retrieval system, or transmitted,
in any form, or by any means, electrical, mechanical, photocopying, recording or otherwise without
the prior written permission of the publisher.

ISBN: 978-1-84780-784-7

Manufactured in Guangdong, China CC092020

18

Photographic acknowledgments (pages 28-29, from left to right) 1. French fashion designer Gabrielle 'Coco' Chanel (1883 - 1971) at a London hotel, 1932 © Keystone Pictures USA / Alamy 2. Coco Chanel, French couturier. Paris, 1936 LIP-283 © Lipnitzki/Roger Viollet/Getty Images 3. Photo © Pictorial Press Ltd / Alamy 4. Photo © Keystone Pictures USA / Alamy

## Collect the Little People, BIG DREAMS® series:

**FRIDA KAHLO**
ISBN: 978-1-84780-783-0

**COCO CHANEL**
ISBN: 978-1-84780-784-7

**MAYA ANGELOU**
ISBN: 978-1-84780-889-9

**AMELIA EARHART**
ISBN: 978-1-84780-888-2

**AGATHA CHRISTIE**
ISBN: 978-1-84780-960-5

**MARIE CURIE**
ISBN: 978-1-84780-962-9

**ROSA PARKS**
ISBN: 978-1-78603-018-4

**AUDREY HEPBURN**
ISBN: 978-1-78603-053-5

**EMMELINE PANKHURST**
ISBN: 978-1-78603-020-7

**ELLA FITZGERALD**
ISBN: 978-1-78603-087-0

**ADA LOVELACE**
ISBN: 978-1-78603-076-4

**JANE AUSTEN**
ISBN: 978-1-78603-120-4

**GEORGIA O'KEEFFE**
ISBN: 978-1-78603-122-8

**HARRIET TUBMAN**
ISBN: 978-1-78603-227-0

**ANNE FRANK**
ISBN: 978-1-78603-229-4

**MOTHER TERESA**
ISBN: 978-1-78603-230-0

**JOSEPHINE BAKER**
ISBN: 978-1-78603-228-7

**L. M. MONTGOMERY**
ISBN: 978-1-78603-233-1

**JANE GOODALL**
ISBN: 978-1-78603-231-7

**SIMONE DE BEAUVOIR**
ISBN: 978-1-78603-232-4

**MUHAMMAD ALI**
ISBN: 978-1-78603-331-4

**STEPHEN HAWKING**
ISBN: 978-1-78603-333-8

**MARIA MONTESSORI**
ISBN: 978-1-78603-755-8

**VIVIENNE WESTWOOD**
ISBN: 978-1-78603-757-2

**MAHATMA GANDHI**
ISBN: 978-1-78603-787-9

**DAVID BOWIE**
ISBN: 978-1-78603-332-1

**WILMA RUDOLPH**
ISBN: 978-1-78603-751-0

**DOLLY PARTON**
ISBN: 978-1-78603-760-2

**BRUCE LEE**
ISBN: 978-1-78603-789-3

**RUDOLF NUREYEV**
ISBN: 978-1-78603-791-6

**ZAHA HADID**

ISBN: 978-1-78603-745-9

**MARY SHELLEY** 
ISBN: 978-1-78603-748-0

**MARTIN LUTHER KING JR.**

ISBN: 978-0-7112-4567-9

**DAVID ATTENBOROUGH**

ISBN: 978-0-7112-4564-8

**ASTRID LINDGREN**

ISBN: 978-0-7112-5217-2

**EVONNE GOOLAGONG**

ISBN: 978-0-7112-4586-0

**BOB DYLAN**

ISBN: 978-0-7112-4675-1

**ALAN TURING**

ISBN: 978-0-7112-4678-2

**BILLIE JEAN KING**

ISBN: 978-0-7112-4693-5

**GRETA THUNBERG**

ISBN: 978-0-7112-5645-3

**JESSE OWENS**

ISBN: 978-0-7112-4583-9

**JEAN-MICHEL BASQUIAT**

ISBN: 978-0-7112-4580-8

**ARETHA FRANKLIN**

ISBN: 978-0-7112-4686-7

**CORAZON AQUINO**

ISBN: 978-0-7112-4684-3

**PELÉ**

ISBN: 978-0-7112-4573-0

**ERNEST SHACKLETON**

ISBN: 978-0-7112-4571-6

**STEVE JOBS**

ISBN: 978-0-7112-4577-8

**AYRTON SENNA**

ISBN: 978-0-7112-4672-0

**LOUISE BOURGEOIS**

ISBN: 978-0-7112-4690-4

**ELTON JOHN**

ISBN: 978-0-7112-5840-2

**JOHN LENNON**

ISBN: 978-0-7112-5767-2

**PRINCE**

ISBN: 978-0-7112-5439-8

**CHARLES DARWIN**

ISBN: 978-0-7112-5771-9

**CAPTAIN TOM MOORE**

ISBN: 978-0-7112-6209-6

**HANS CHRISTIAN ANDERSEN**

ISBN: 978-0-7112-5934-8

# ACTIVITY BOOKS

**STICKER ACTIVITY BOOK**

ISBN: 978-0-7112-6012-2

**COLORING BOOK**

ISBN: 978-0-7112-6136-5

**LITTLE ME, BIG DREAMS JOURNAL**

ISBN: 978-0-7112-4889-2